A PRACTICAL GUIDE FOR FAMILIES & INDIVIDUALS

TO ACHIEVE FINANCIAL EMPOWERMENT, ECONOMIC GROWTH & ECONOMIC STABILITY

AUBREY WALCOTT, SR., MS, MBA

DEMBA
FINANCIAL
SOLUTIONS
LLC

A Publication of

DEMBA
FINANCIAL
SOLUTIONS
LLC

P.O. Box 4231
Silver Spring, MD 20914
Visit our web site at
http://www.dembafinancialsolutions.net

Book Design and Cover Illustration
© 2014 Gloria Marconi Illustration & Design

Printed in the United States of America

ISBN 978-1501046636

This book is designed to provide competent and reliable information regarding the
subject matters covered. However, it is sold with the understanding that the author and
publisher are not engaged in rendering investment, professional or legal advice. Laws
and practices often vary from state to state, and if expert assistance is required, the
service of a professional should be sought. The author and publisher specifically disclaim
any liability that is incurred from the use or application of the contents of this book.

The case history discussed in *A Practical Guide for Families and Individuals to
Achieve Financial Empowerment, Economic Growth and Economic Stability* is true.
However, the names and other identifying characteristics have been changed to protect
the privacy of individuals.

ACKNOWLEDGEMENTS

This book on financial literacy is dedicated to teaching families and individuals, the practical ways to achieve financial empowerment, economic growth and economic stability in their lives.

In addition, the basic financial principles provided in this book–when applied–will immediately serve to transform the lives of families and individuals living under desperate financial circumstances.

A special thanks to Leah Smith for her invaluable contribution in providing her precious time to review changes and assist in making corrections as the book was being written.

TABLE OF CONTENTS

INTRODUCTION

This book is written as a practical guide for families and individuals who have a vested interest in improving and maintaining a solid financial position. The financial strategies and advice offered in this book, if implemented step by step, will serve families and individuals for generations. A key strategy of this book is to assist families and individuals to move forward with creating intergenerational wealth.

Given the permanent economic challenges faced by families and individuals in today's society, particularly in the areas of housing insecurity, employment insecurity, high cost of education and a challenging and changing health care environment, it is important to build your financial position on a strong foundation.

The principles enumerated in this book will entail some level of sacrifice on the part of families and individuals desirous of achieving solid financial success. This book provides a road map for families and individuals to reach their financial goals. It also provides the principles and methodologies to build a strong financial position in a changing economic and political environment.

This book is written in simple language for easy reading. Persistent application of the principles and strategies enumerated in this book show families and individuals, simple and practical ways to dramatically and permanently improve their respective financial positions.

CHAPTER 1

SAVING FOR THE FUTURE

Financial literacy is the tool that will assist families and individuals to move from facing a poverty existence to achieving a life time of permanent financial independence and success. In our current economic situation it is important for families and individuals living from pay check to pay check, and on the brink of financial disaster, to carefully evaluate their financial situation, and take immediate steps to reverse the inevitable outcome; a permanent slide into crushing poverty. This common sense, practical book shows families and individuals how to become financially successful.

In this chapter our discussion centers on the strategies for effective personal savings. The key focus is on personal savings, retirement savings, health savings accounts, flexible spending accounts and insurance products.

PERSONAL SAVINGS

The principle hedge against financial failure for families and individuals is personal savings. Therefore, it is imperative that a permanent practical budget and a savings plan be in place to achieve a measured financial outcome to deal with all life challenges.

- **Principle 1: How to Start Saving Effortlessly** *Paying yourself first before anyone else is the key to personal savings.* To achieve rapid success, your personal savings has to be automatic. Review your budget and determine the amount of money you can comfortably save monthly. It could be a modest amount of $5, $10, $15, $20 or $25. After you have determined the amount you want to save, simply sign up for automatic payroll deductions with your payroll office at your job, and have that amount deducted from your pay check automatically and sent to your bank or credit union. I would advise that you do not get an Automatic Teller Machine (ATM) card. ATM cards make it too easy for you to access and spend your savings. Limiting unnecessary withdrawals will allow your savings to grow and be available for your use in the event of an emergency. Your emergency fund should be a significant amount of money to cover 36 months of living and miscellaneous expenses; because you do not know what life-changing events you may experience.

- **Principle 2: Time Factor of Money** The compounding effect of money allows your savings to grow year after year if a level of consistency is maintained. It is counterproductive to save more money than you can afford because you will never reach your financial goals. You should increase the amount of your personal savings with every salary increase you receive.

- **Principle 3: Retirement Savings Accounts** It is imperative that you participate in your company's retirement savings program if one is available. You do not want to leave any free money on the table provided by your employer. You want to

2

maximize your retirement savings by saving enough money to get the company's match. Remember, savings should always be automatic; it helps you to reach your financial goals faster. Authorize your payroll office to deduct the percentage amount you want to save; 5% to 6% is a good starting point. Again, every time you receive a pay raise, increase the percentage you are saving.

BRIEF EXPLANATION OF RETIREMENT PLANS

- **Defined Benefit Plan** is the traditional retirement plan that companies used to offer their employees. Based on a tax model of five years or ten years of employment with that company, you became vested in the retirement plan without contributing a penny of your own money. In other words, as a benefit to you the company puts aside money for your retirement. However, those days are gone. A high percentage of companies have eliminated this employee benefit.

- **Defined Contribution Plan** is the popular 401(k) retirement savings plan that 90% of all companies are offering their employees. Employees are now expected to save for their own retirement by contributing pre tax dollars (before taxes are taken out of your pay check) to their 401(k) retirement savings plans. The company may offer a matched amount of fifty cents for every dollar you contribute at a 6% level to your retirement savings. It is imperative that you save whatever percentage amount you can, even if the percentage amount does not qualify for the company's match. Keep focusing on the fact that you are solely responsible and accountable for saving money for your retirement.

SOCIAL SECURITY BENEFITS

Social Security benefits are available to all American citizens who

3

qualify. You can draw Social Security benefits at age sixty two or you can wait and draw benefits at age sixty five or at age seventy if you so choose. ***Contact the Social Security Administration for more information.***

HEALTH SAVINGS ACCOUNTS

This is a savings vehicle for families and individuals with large incomes who can afford to pay high deductible costs for medical treatment in exchange for a lower premium. If the money contributed is not used, it is rolled over year after year and keeps accumulating until used for medical expenses. The current maximum contribution for 2014 is $5,000 for individuals and married couples filing a joint tax return, and $2,500 for a married couple filing separate tax returns. If you are a high earner this is also a good way for you to save more money and reduce your tax liability.

4

FLEXIBLE SAVINGS ACCOUNTS

This is a savings vehicle for families and individuals. The contribution amount for 2014 for individuals is $3,300 per year. The contribution for families is $6,550 per year. This money can only be used for incidental medical expenses: such as eye glasses, drugs, dental work etc. The only down side to flexible savings accounts is that the amount of money not used by a specific date is forfeited. This is a good account to have because it helps you to pay for miscellaneous medical expenses. However, you need to be vigilant and use every penny before the expiration date or you will lose the money contributed to this account.

INSURANCE

Insurance is a financial instrument that provides a hedge against unforeseen risks. Therefore, you purchase insurance products ahead of time before you have a need to use the product.

If you have a family that depends upon your income for daily living, you should buy life insurance. The insurance product you should purchase is term life insurance to provide significant financial support for your family should anything happen to you. Do not purchase insurance products such as whole life or universal insurance policies. In addition, to protect yourself financially you need to buy the following insurance products: such as car insurance, health insurance, renter's insurance, homeowner's insurance and disability insurance.

STUDENT LOANS

Families and individuals should take the time to analyze the long term impact of student loans on their financial position before borrowing to finance their college education. The exponential increases in the cost of higher education coupled with stagnant wages and salaries should be concerning to all of us. If you are a middle class family, your first options should be to send your child to your in-state community colleges and universities to save on college costs and student loans. Make certain that your child is enrolled in a program that will bring a solid return on your investment (ROI) after graduation from college.

Excessive student loan debt can be detrimental to families' and individuals' financial and economic position. In addition, you should always remember that student loan debt–like taxes–must be paid. These debts are not dischargeable under bankruptcy. Families and individuals with young children could start saving for their children's college education early by investing in their state's 529 College Savings Program. Families and individuals should save for retirement first before saving for college.

5

6

CHAPTER 2

BUYING ON CREDIT AND DEBT

O ne of the most destructive financial instruments that has caused severe pain for families and individuals is the credit card. As the economy gets tougher, families and individuals are faced with employment insecurity, lack of job promotions and layoffs that have become the new normal in our society. We have seen the difficulties families and individuals have faced in dealing with national credit cards such as Visa® and MasterCard®, revolving charge accounts, buying strategies, credit card management, credit card payments, carrying multiple credit cards, debt avoidance, credit life insurance and payday loans. These are just some of the confusing choices that bombard consumers as they try to make ends meet.

CREDIT CARDS

National credit cards such as Visa® or MasterCard®, or a credit card from a local credit union are very good financial instruments to have in your possession. However, these credit cards can be dangerous to your financial well-being if they are not used prudently. The following rule of thumb should apply when selecting a credit card:

1. **Select a credit card with a reputable bank or credit union** that offers the lowest interest rate along with good customer service.

2. **Avoid enticing advertisements from banks** that send promotional materials asking you to transfer your credit card balance to a credit card they are offering at a low introductory interest rate. If you cannot read and understand the legal language in the offer being made, and you sign up to receive the new credit card, you may find that you have made a horrible mistake that could cost you lots of money. Also, make sure to shred any of these offers before throwing them in the trash. Identity thieves can use these offers to apply for credit with your information and make purchases.

3. **Avoid rewards credit card offers from airlines, banks and credit card companies.** Keep in mind that these cards make lots of money for the companies that issue them, and you the consumer receive very little benefit in return. For example, if you travel a lot and you decide to get an airline travel reward credit card you could reap lots of benefits. However, if you do not travel a lot it is futile to have one of these cards because you will receive no benefits.

4. **Avoid revolving credit card offers from department stores.** The interest rates on these cards are just too high. Be aware of the promotional pitch from the sales staff telling you that you can save an additional 20% to 50% on your purchases if you open an account with the store. Always decline these offers and use only cash or your major credit card to make purchases.

5. Credit Buying Strategies:

- *Always remember that cash is king.* Use cash to pay for your items instead of creating a bill with principle and interest that you will have to pay at the end of the month or in installments to close that transaction.

- *Use your credit wisely, and avoid impulse buying at all costs.* Your credit card is a line of credit extended to you by the credit card company. There are risks and obligations associated with using the credit card. Payment in full or in installment amounts is demanded upon receipt of a bill. *Take advantage of the interest free loan you receive every time you use your credit card by paying your bill in full at the end of the billing cycle.*

- *Stagger your credit card purchases* to avoid being hit with different interest rates. Pay off your old balance before incurring new charges.

9

CREDIT CARD MANAGEMENT STRATEGIES

1. **Limit yourself to no more than two credit cards** per family or individual. Be aware, too many credit cards can lower your credit score.

2. **One of your credit cards should always have a zero balance** for emergency use only.

3. **To get the maximum benefits from your credit card, the balance should be paid in full monthly.** If you cannot pay your balance in full you are not managing your money very well, and should discontinue using your credit card until your financial situation improves.

4. **Always remember that good old cash is always king,**

and is accepted everywhere as a medium of exchange.

5. **Never give anyone access to your credit card.** If your credit card is not stolen you are fully responsible for all charges made to your credit card.

6. **If you cannot make payment on your credit card** as agreed per the contract you signed, please notify your credit card company as soon as possible. There may be programs in place to assist you to avoid deeper credit problems. Do not make the mistake of allowing a family member or friend to make charges to your credit card with the promise to pay later. In the event that you allow someone to use your credit card please get the person to sign a written agreement acknowledging the use of your credit card to make purchases and the date payment is expected. If you have to seek redress from the courts this document will be invaluable in supporting your claim.

7. **Never use a credit card to pay off another credit card.** You could do irreparable damage to your credit.

10

SECURED CREDIT CARD

If you are having credit challenges, and want to improve your credit and credit score, you can apply for *a Secured Credit Card from a credit union or bank.* You will deposit your own money into a savings account; the amount could be $200 or $5,000 to secure the credit card and guarantee payment of charges. The key is to make every monthly payment on time. After you have made on time payments for 12 months the bank could convert you to a regular credit card customer. The beauty of having a secured credit card is that you can use it to make purchases just like a regular credit card. Only you and the bank are aware of the type of credit card you are using to make hotel reservations and rent cars.

DEBT AVOIDANCE

It is imperative that families and individuals grasp the significance of effective money management. The concepts of planning and budgeting are not foreign concepts and should not be taken lightly. Therefore, families and individuals must learn how to successfully employ the tools of planning and budgeting to reach their goals of financial empowerment, economic growth and economic stability. Understanding the concept of need verses want in the decision making process is very critical to avoiding debt.

In life when you fail to plan, you are planning to fail. Therefore, for families and individuals to significantly improve their financial and economic status they must incorporate the concept of planning in their daily lives. Employing the simple principles of budgeting allows for effective control of your finances, and provides a solid base from which to approach life's challenges and make sound financial decisions.

11

FULFILLING A WANT

A want is not a need. You may want to buy a product you saw advertised on television. Before you purchase this product you may want to ask yourself "what is the intrinsic value of this product to my household?" then analyze your budget, which is the key to your buying decisions. If you cannot determine the usefulness of this product to your household, it should not be purchased.

FULFILLING A NEED

A need is a much more obvious void that exists in families and individuals lives. For example, if your family does not have a car and one is needed to get to and from work because of a lack of public transportation that is a pressing need that has to be filled. However, despite this need the budget analysis process must be exercised, before a final decision is made to make a purchase. Prudent spending is the hallmark of financial stability.

CREDIT LIFE INSURANCE

Many credit card companies, banks, credit unions, finance companies, and large department and furniture stores will offer you credit life insurance when you get a credit card or extension of credit. *You should never check the box on the application accepting credit life insurance.* This is not a good deal for you the customer. It benefits only the companies.

CREDIT COUNSELING

Crediting counseling is an invaluable service offered to families and individuals who are overwhelmed with debt. *The Consumer Federation of America* has offices throughout the country that provide credit counseling services free of charge. This service is also offered by financial professionals in the credit field for a fee. A credit counseling professional is able to work with your creditors to consolidate your debt, and give you the opportunity to make one single monthly payment towards paying off your debt. Consult a credit counselor if you are having financial problems.

PAYDAY LOANS / NO CREDIT LOANS

Payday Loan Companies should be avoided with every fiber of your being. These are predatory lenders that prey on innocent families and individuals who have credit challenges and are in need of financial assistance. These companies charge very high interest rates and high fees. You could end up owing thousands of dollars more than the original amount you contracted for if you are not vigilant, or have a clear understanding of the financial contract to which you have obligated yourself. If you need a loan and your immediate family, close friends or relatives cannot help, seek out a credit union. Credit unions usually have the lowest interest rates and affordable repayment plans.

You can also contact a bank to see if you qualify for a signature or a collateral loan. Always keep in mind that the annual percentage rate (APR) estimated on a payday loan can be as high as 700% to a 1000%. The high cost of a payday loan should prevent you from seeking to obtain such a loan, and propel you in another direction. If you choose this route, you will be paying a high rate of interest, which means that your expenses will increase. However, if getting a payday loan is your only option to deal with your financial situation, please make certain it is a onetime only option, and pay it off as quickly as possible.

PRODUCT WARRANTIES & MAINTENANCE CONTRACTS

When you buy a washing machine, dryer, television, computer, car or a grill–just to mention a few products–you will be approached with a hard sell to purchase an extended warranty. ***These warranties are not worth the paper they are written on and should never be purchased.*** Remember that all products of this type will come with a manufacturer's warranty for at least one year sometime even two years. Always register your product with the company. This can be done online or by filling out the registration card. Companies are making billions of dollars a year selling warranties to unsuspecting customers. Always decline these offers. Companies will also try to sell you a maintenance contract at the time of your purchase. Remember the manufacturer's warranty should take care of anything that goes wrong with the product in the first or second year.

CREDIT BUREAUS

There are three credit bureau companies that everyone needs to become familiar with.

EQUIFAX	EXPERIAN	TRANSUNION
1-800-525-6285	1-888-379-3742	1-800-680-7289
P.O. Box 740241	P.O. Box 9532	P.O. Box 6790
Atlanta, GA 30374-0241	Allen, Texas 75013	Fullerton, CA 92831
www.equifax.com	www.experian.com	www.transunion.com

The credit bureaus store all of your credit transactions. Every time you apply for credit to purchase a house, to purchase a car, to get a credit card, and for employment, one or all three credit bureaus may be contacted by the credit grantor to see if you have the capacity and the willingness to pay for your purchases. Employers are also looking at your credit report to get a character profile on you before making an employment decision. Companies can report positive and negative information on you to the credit bureaus. Because of the high levels of mistakes in credit reports, and the prevalence of identity theft occurring in society today, it is incumbent upon everyone to be vigilant by reviewing their credit reports regularly.

You can get an annual free copy of your credit report from all three credit bureaus by just going on line at www.annualcreditreport.com. You should also get a copy of your credit score from Fair Isaac Corporation. This score is used by creditors to determine your credit worthiness, and whether to grant you credit.

UNDERSTANDING BANKRUPTCY

Filing for bankruptcy for many families and individuals has a negative connotation. However, if you are overwhelmed with debt, and cannot make significant improvements in debt reduction you may find that filing for bankruptcy protection could bring you significant financial and psychological relief. Businesses with significant debt file for bankruptcy protection frequently to protect their assets and gain relief from their creditors. Therefore, families and individuals should not be afraid to take advantage of this legal remedy to become financially solvent.

There are several types of bankruptcy, but the two that would be applicable to individuals are the following: *Chapter 7, and Chapter 13. Consult with a bankruptcy attorney to get advice on which one would be best for your particular financial situation.* Once your bankruptcy has been approved by the court, it will be entered into your credit bureau report, and it will stay there for 10 years. Use you new financial freedom to rebuild your credit and financial position. *Do not have any discussions or sign any papers with your creditors after your bankruptcy has been approved by the court.*

15

COLLECTION AGENCIES

If you are being hounded by an unscrupulous collection agency to pay a bill that is not yours, you should contact the Consumer Financial Protection Board, which is charged with the responsibility of regulating collection agencies and protecting consumers against unscrupulous companies. You can also refer to the *Fair Debt Collections Act* that governs the practices and conduct of collection agencies. If you owe a legitimate debt, pay that debt! If you cannot pay all of the debt, make payment arrangements with your creditor. Be aware that because of the current economic situation, companies are referring customers' accounts to collection agencies and selling accounts to factoring companies much sooner than six months. Employ the following strategies when dealing with a collection agency or company attempting to collect a debt:

1. **If you are receiving collection calls at work** from a collection agency, you can request to not be called at work. This is a provision of the Fair Debt Collection Act.

2. **Calls made to your home after 8:00 PM** are in violation of the Fair Debt Collection Act.

3. **Keep logs of every conversation** you have with a representative from a collection agency or company attempting to collect a debt. *Record the name of the person with whom you spoke, the time and date of the call, the caller's phone number and the content of your conversation.*

4. **Respond to every correspondence** you receive from the collection agency in writing via registered mail, and request a receipt of delivery. Limit your telephone conversations with representatives of the agency because many times they are not properly documented, and the turnover of employees in the debt collection profession is very high.

5. **You have 30 days** from the date you receive a letter demanding payment from a collection agency to either pay or dispute the debt.

6. **Collection agencies on most occasions will only send you a summary** bill requesting payment of the debt. Do not ignore the letter from the collection agency. Respond in writing via registered mail requesting delivery receipt. Request the following information from the collection agency so that you can verify that the debt is yours.

   • *The name of creditor such as a merchant, financial institution or service provider and their address*

   • *Date merchandise was purchased or service provided*

   • *Itemized bill of merchandise purchased or service provided*

   Do not rush to pay a bill that may not be yours or a bill that is in dispute because of an error made by the merchant or service provider

If you are sued by the collection agency or the company to which you owe a debt, take the following actions:

- *Keep your court date* so that you can defend yourself against the suit. If you owe the debt you may be able to get a court approved payment plan to pay off your debt after you have shown the court evidence of why you have been unable to pay. If you do not owe the debt, you can present your evidence to the court disputing the collection agency's claim.

- *THIS NOTE IS VERY IMPORTANT. If you do not go to court to defend yourself against the suit, a default judgment will be entered against you by the court.*

- *If the court enters a default judgment against you* the collection agency is then able to garnish your paycheck or take money out of your bank account if it is accessible.

If you are in a dispute with a merchant or service provider, document your credit file by sending a written letter of the dispute to the three credit bureaus to be attached to your credit report.

18

CHAPTER 3

MAKING LOANS TO OTHERS

L ending money is a phenomenon that has created bitterness and conflict among families and individuals since time immemorial. Should you lend money to anyone? Before you do, consider the risks and challenges, and how this transaction could affect your relationship with that individual or your financial position. In this chapter the focus is on the strategies that will allow families and individuals to keep their hard earned money in their possession.

LENDING MONEY

Lending money is a habit you should never engage in with family, friends, or acquaintances. Lending money has risks and consequences and challenges beyond your control, and could hurt you financially and psychologically. If anyone asks to borrow money from you your answer should be a resounding *"No!"* If you can afford it, I would suggest the following strategy. If the borrower is requesting $200, I would suggest you give no more than $20, and let the borrower know that he/she does not have to pay it back. ***Do not become someone else's ATM.*** It is not your responsibility to financially provide for anyone outside of your immediate family, your spouse and children. Everyone else such as siblings, aunts, uncles, nephews, nieces, fathers and mothers, domestic partners, dating partners, friends and associates should contact a financial institution such as a bank or credit union or other financial institutions for a loan. Adults who are gainfully employed should save some of their money for emergencies, so that if an emergency occurs they can go to the bank and get the money they need, and should not be depending on others. Remember if you lose a friend to whom you refused to lend money, that person was not your friend in the first place.

20 PROMISSORY NOTE

Never lend money without a signed promissory note. It is important to note that money changing hands without the force of legal protection is a bad idea. If you are asked by someone for a loan protect yourself by insisting that the person signs a promissory note that states the terms of the loan and the repayment date. ***If the person refuses to sign the promissory note, do not give that person a loan.*** When lending to any one do not provide them with cash. Use a check or money order and note in the memo section that the funds being distributed is a loan, so that you will have a physical record of the transaction along with the promissory note. If you have to go to court to recover your money these documents will be invaluable in proving your claim. A sample copy of a promissory note is in the Appendix Section of this book.

CO-SIGNING DOCUMENTS

You should never co-sign documents for anyone. It is imperative that you consider the financial implications and the potential credit challenges that could arise as a result of co-signing for another person to obtain credit to buy or lease a car, rent a house or an apartment. If this person has credit challenges and could not qualify on their own for credit, and you co-sign the contract documents with that person, you become the primary person responsible and liable for the debt. If the person you co-signed for is in default of the contractual agreement for non-payment of the financial obligation, you will be sued if you cannot pay off the contractual obligation. *Protect your credit and your financial position. Do not co-sign for anyone.*

DATING COUPLES

If you are in a dating relationship, you should be very vigilant with your finances. To avoid being taken advantage of or swindled by financial predators who are looking for an easy ride in life, *your wallet, credit cards, bank accounts to include checking and savings and your investment accounts should never be a part of any financial discussions.* Many of us make the mistake of letting our guard down after a few dates, and expose our financial position to people who do not have our best interest at heart. Do not become a victim of financial fraud. Be smart, have fun, keep your eyes open, protect your finances and grow rich.

MARRIED COUPLES

It is important that married couples be cognizant of the financial transactions occurring in their daily lives, and how their financial plans and savings can be affected. In today's society, financial decisions should not be left to just one person in a union. Both partners–even grown children–should be involved in discussions of financial matters pertaining to the family. As families make life changing financial decisions such as dealing with the cost of college, buying a new car, taking a vacation, buying a new home for a growing family or just making significant repairs to their current home, it is incumbent upon the family to analyze their budget and perform a cost/benefit analysis to make the right financial decisions. For example, if you have a car that is ten years old, and it is in need of significant repairs in the amount of $7,000, but the *Kelly Blue Book* value for the car is only $2,000 what will be your decision? After doing the financial analysis your decision should be to get rid of the car. No one in his/her right mind will spend $7,000 to repair a car that is only worth $2,000. Spend the time to do the analysis and make the right financial decision that will benefit you and your family financially.

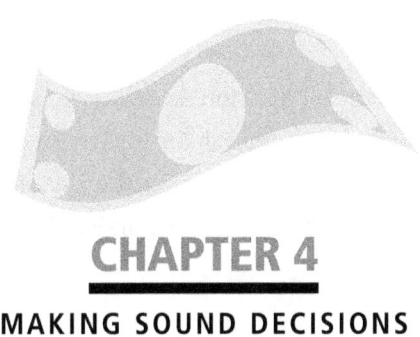

CHAPTER 4

MAKING SOUND DECISIONS

To illuminate the challenges faced by families and individuals in the financial decision making process, the focus of this chapter will be instructive on the principles of practical and emotional decision making. The decisions that families and individuals make in the short run can become a lifelong burden financially, emotionally and psychologically.

PRACTICAL DECISION MAKING

The principles of practical decision making encompasses the use of the following tools to make sound financial decisions:

1. **Budget Analysis**

2. **Savings Availability**

3. **Credit Availability**

4. **How does the financial decision affect the family or individual?**

Before any financial decision is made it is important that the decision maker conduct an analysis of his/her budget. Performing an analysis of the budget will provide you the decision maker with the numbers needed to make a sound financial decision.

EMOTIONAL DECISION MAKING

Decisions made without proper analysis based in fact and without good data could result in serious consequences and have a negative impact on the financial empowerment, economic growth and economic stability of families and individuals. It is always prudent to make financial decisions with facts and data associated with your budget, savings and credit availability. This principle of decision making allows the decision maker to gauge the financial impact on the family or individual.

Financial decisions made in haste are always considered to be an emotional decision. To build financial empowerment, economic growth and economic stability, families and individuals must avoid the pitfalls of making emotional financial decisions. A key strategy for families and individuals to employ to mitigate the risk in emotional decision making, is never to make one. However, if you feel compelled to make a purchase, please employ the principle of practical decision making, and strive vigilantly to abandon emotional financial decision making.

PSYCHOLOGICAL EFFECT OF EMOTIONAL
FINANCIAL DECISION MAKING

A bad financial decision can have a devastating impact on the mental state of families and individuals. Despite the prognostication of economic experts and government officials that the economy is recovering rapidly, these statements do not compute with the high levels of job insecurity, rising housing foreclosure rates, high unemployment, stagnant salaries, rising cost of education and continued challenges with accessing health care for citizens. Therefore, families and individuals have to make financial decisions predicated on the economic factors driving their lives in this current economic and political environment.

Avoiding the pitfalls of emotional financial decision making may reduce to some degree the stress in your daily life. The psychological effect of emotional decision making could cause families and individuals to spend more of their hard earned money to correct decisions that could have been avoided with a little planning and analysis. Always strive to keep the pendulum swinging in the financial growth position, and pay attention to how you are managing your finances.

26

CHAPTER 5

REDUCING EXTRAVAGANT SPENDING

F amilies and individuals striving to reach their financial goals have to get serious and avoid the extravagant spending habits that affects most of us. We live in a consumer-driven society, and we are bombarded daily with numerous advertisements of various products to purchase. Many families and individuals fall victim to this barrage of advertisements and make bad purchasing decisions with their hard earned money, suffering financial ruin as a result of emotional spending.

Families and individuals should work to stop extravagant spending by following these principles:

1. Strive to live simply and below your financial means.
If you make $40,000 annually live on $30,000, and save the remaining $10,000. An example of prudent spending would be to visit local thrift stores for gently used, pre-owned items such as clothing or household goods. If you are a careful shopper, you can find what you need at a fraction of the cost of regular

retail stores. This allows families and individuals to have more discretionary income to meet other living expenses.

2. Create a budget that will help guide your spending habits.

3. Do you want to be financially prosperous and rich? If the answer is yes, then stop spending your hard earned money to make others wealthy. Be selfish and save your money so that you can join the ranks of the wealthy.

INCREASE ASSETS ACCUMULATION

Families and individuals should strive to increase their assets accumulation by every legal means necessary. The strategies for accomplishing this goal are as follows:

1. Obtain as much education and credentials as you possibly can.

2. Establish a personal savings account at a bank or credit union with automatic savings deductions.

3. Establish retirement accounts at your place of employment. If you are self-employed, make every effort to have a personal savings account. In addition, if you are self-employed you can also establish a 401(k) retirement plan account specifically designated for self-employed individuals.

4. Buy a home or an income-producing property as soon you can afford it. Get the benefits of living in your own home, plus the benefits of mortgage interest and energy deductions to reduce your taxes. I would recommend that you purchase as many properties as you can afford to solidify your assets accumulation and grow your wealth. The three most important measures when you are buying a home is the size of your down payment, your credit score and your ability to make the monthly payments.

5. Buy US bonds particularly the E Series bonds, which have an inflation protector.

When you buy a house, or get a good education, these are assets that will appreciate in value over time. The stability of these assets will certainly help families and individuals to grow financially strong, and start the journey of achieving financial empowerment, economic growth and economic stability.

Spending your hard earned money on material things that depreciate in value is not beneficial for families or individuals. If this practice is not curtailed, it could lead to a quick decent into the bowels of crushing poverty. Please be mindful of how much money you spend on items all of us use every day in our lives such as cars, furniture, clothing, vacations and electronic equipment. All of these items serve a useful purpose, but you cannot count on any of these items to build wealth for you because they all depreciate in value. For instance, as soon as you drive off the dealer's lot with you new car it depreciates by 25%.

29

KEEPING YOUR WEALTH HIDDEN

Your wealth should be kept hidden. Do not flaunt your wealth with extravagant purchases, exotic vacations and throwing luxurious parties to show others that you have made it financially; it may come back to bite you. *A large number of wealthy people do not have expensive things; that is, in fact, the reason they are wealthy.* Spending thousands of dollars on rims for you cars, fur coats and boats are an outward manifestation of how you want your peers and others to view you. This buying charade is not necessary and should be stopped. *For example, look at Warren Buffet: he is a billionaire who can afford anything he wants, but he still lives in the same house he bought before becoming wealthy.* You can be wealthy and live simply. Families and individuals who have achieved financial wealth should strive to keep it hidden in a bank and not on display for the public to see.

AVOIDING BANK OVERDRAFT CHARGES

When you open a checking account with a bank, you will be offered overdraft protection. You should decline this overdraft protection offer. Banks make billions of dollars from the overdraft protection services they offer to their customers. If you write a check for $100 and the money is not in your account, with overdraft protection the bank will pay the check by advancing you a loan at significant interest. You will then have to pay back to the bank the amount that was loaned to you. This means that every time you make a deposit to your account, the bank will take their loan payment out first.

30

Writing bounced checks is not only expensive, it is illegal. *To avoid having to pay your bank for overdraft protection, link your savings account to your checking account and this should eliminate the need for an overdraft plan with your bank.* You must fund your savings account to avoid any bounced check fees charged by the bank for processing an insufficient funds check. The cost of a bounced check could be $25 to $40, depending on the policy of the financial institution. If you were automatically enrolled in your bank's overdraft protection plan, you can opt out by asking your bank to remove your account from this service.

Remember, it is your responsibility to reconcile your checking account monthly to make certain that you have the funds available when you write a check or use your debit card to make purchases. A good habit is to use the check register provided with your checks to record every transaction associated with your purchases and debit card withdrawals.

Hundreds of thousands of dollars are wasted each year by families and individuals who, for whatever reason, do not use their own bank's

ATM to get cash. If you want to get rich, you have to be able to save pennies before you can save dollars. *Stop the bad habit of throwing your money away, by paying another bank to get your own money.* Make it your business to know the locations of your bank's ATMs, and get your cash there. Every dollar you can save brings you closer to your goal of achieving financial independence. *Before using any ATM, look for skimming devices that may be attached to the section where you input your card, or cameras over the key pad where you enter your pin number. There are thieves trying to get your ATM card information so they can steal your hard earned money. Always be vigilant and aware of your surroundings whenever you are using an ATM.*

CREDIT CARD BALANCE TRANSFER FEES

31

You should *never* accept a credit card that requires you to pay a balance transfer fee. However, if you have a credit card with a very high interest rate, calculate the amount of the transfer fee (usually 3%) versus how much you could save in interest, before making this kind of decision.

32

CHAPTER 6

BUYING STRATEGIES FOR MAJOR PURCHASES

Families and individuals should be aware of the financial pitfalls when making large purchases, and strive to keep more of their hard earned money in their bank accounts.

STRATEGIES WHEN BUYING A CAR

When buying a car or other vehicles apply the following principles:

1. **It is wise to get pre-approved first by your bank or credit union** for a car loan. Your financial institution will determine the loan amount you can afford and the conditions of the loan. Do not turn your financing over to the car dealer because you will pay thousands of dollars more for that vehicle. It is a good possibility that you may leave the dealership owing more than the car is worth. Keep in mind that a new car loses 25% of its value as soon as you drive it off the dealer's lot.

2. **Always analyze the advertised interest percentage for financing a car** and the rebate amount offered by the

car dealer. You can save lots of money by looking at the rebate amount being offered verses the interest percentage. The benefit of the rebate amount offered is that it reduces the price of the car and lowers your monthly payments. Do not just look at the interest rate on the car look at the whole package and then make your decision.

3. **The two most important contract documents you will sign when purchasing a car are the Motor Vehicle Contract of Sale and the Retail Installment Contract.** *The Motor Vehicle Contract of Sale* obligates you to buy the vehicle. *The Retail Installment Contract* obligates you to the loan. Signing both of these contract documents obligates you to pay for the vehicle. If you were pre-approved for a loan from your bank or credit union, you do not have to sign the Retail Installment Contract. Never sign blank or duplicate contracts or other paperwork. Always protect yourself by reading the documents carefully prior to signing. Do not sign any documents until you are ready to make a firm decision on your purchase. Please get copies of the documents you have signed for your records. Always remember that you have three business days to cancel a contract.

4. **Review your contract** to make certain that the numbers are correct, and that you are not being charged for items you did not agree to purchase. The simple way to accomplish this action is to take the final dollar number at the bottom of the contract and add your down payment; the amount you get is what it will cost you to buy the car. To remove unwanted items or question some of your initial choices subtract every amount on the contract by item from this amount until you get the final amount you want to pay for the car.

BUYING A CAR VERSUS REPAIRING A CAR

Families and individuals should analyze the need for repairing or buying a car. If your car has sustained significant damage your first thought may be to get it repaired. However, if you do a proper analysis you may find that the *Kelly Blue Book* value for the car is less than the damage sustained by the vehicle. Therefore, if the car is worth $1,000 per *Kelly Blue Book* and the damage is $4,000 this car should not be repaired. You should sell the car and use the proceeds to purchase another vehicle.

REAL ESTATE RENTALS

When renting an apartment, read and understand your lease. Your lease is the contractual document that governs the landlord's rights and your legal rights and conditions to occupy the apartment. Be aware that the landlord is not responsible for any of your personal property that may be lost through fire, water damage or theft. You need to get you own renters' insurance to protect your personal property. The landlord does not offer this protection for you, the renter. The insurance the landlord has protects his property only. Replacing all of the possessions that you have accumulated over the years could be financially challenging. The cost of renters' insurance is reasonable. For a $30,000 policy, your monthly cost could be $60. Get the peace of mind you deserve knowing that you are financially protected against any unforeseen disasters.

VACATION MONEY PITFALLS

When you take a vacation with your family, strive to have a wonderful and enjoyable time. Unfortunately, vacation packages are stacked with a lot of promotional advertisements. One of the biggest gimmicks is providing you with a large dollar credit amount that you can use while you are at the resort. However, before you can use this credit, you are subjected to hours of a sales seminar trying to entice you into signing a contract to purchase a time share apartment in their properties. *Remember, in the USA under the Uniform Commercial Code you have three days to rescind a contract before it goes into effect.* I doubt that the same legal protection is available in other countries. Be careful! Do not saddle yourself and your family with unnecessary expenses by signing a contract for a time share property during your vacation. It is very difficult to sell your stake in a time share and the ongoing maintenance fees could be very high.

STRATEGIES TO EMPLOY WHEN BUYING A HOUSE

When purchasing a home, please follow these simple principles:

36

1. **Employ a buyer's real estate agent to represent you solely.** Always remember that real estate agents represent the seller and not the buyer. Therefore, if you want someone to look out for your interest a buyer's agent is a must.

2. **Review your credit score** to make certain that you have no negative issues in your credit record.

3. **Get pre-approved for a loan** from your financial institution.

4. **The lowest interest rate you can get is par.** Ask your loan officer for the par rate.

5. **Get a Good Faith Estimate for a 30-year loan.** This estimate should list comprehensively all of the costs for the loan including principal, interest, taxes and escrow amount. Pay close attention to the fees being charged including the Paid Out of Closing amount (POC) or the back end commission amount charged to your loan known as Yield Spread Premium Amount. Make certain that you do not have a prepayment clause in your contract. Make certain that you do not have a balloon clause in your contract. Try to get a loan without private mortgage insurance.

6. **Do not buy a home you cannot afford.** Get the lowest possible price for the home through negotiations. The important things to remember are that lenders are looking for buyers that can demonstrate the *capacity* and *willingness* to purchase a home. Capacity is measured by the size of your down payment and your ability to make the monthly mortgage payments. Willingness is a demonstration of how timely you have made payments on your current and past financial obligations.

7. **Closely review your HUD1 closing document** before signing. Request a copy of the closing documents three days before closing on your house. Discuss any excessive or junk fees with your loan officer and agent and get them removed. You will have so many contract documents to sign, that it will prevent you from doing a thorough review of the contract at closing time.

37

STRATEGIES TO EMPLOY WHEN REFINANCING YOUR HOME

Refinancing your home can bring relief from crushing debt, and at the same time relieve you of some, or all of your equity you have built up in your home over the years. You need to protect your home equity from unscrupulous loan officers who want to strip you of the equity you have in your home. Please remember that a loan officer is only interested in lining his/her own pocket with the fees that come from your loan. The loan officer is not looking out for your best interest. Therefore, it is your responsibility–and in your best interest–to understand the refinancing process. Do not be swayed by glib advertisements, phone calls, solicitation letters or email from your mortgage servicer, or other financial institutions offering you a deal to refinance your home.

You could be vulnerable to refinancing your home if you have the following credit challenges:

1. Extremely high credit card balances

2. Your credit card payments are late

3. Collectors are calling because of nonpayment of outstanding balances

4. You want a lower mortgage payment

5. You have a back log of home improvement projects that needs to be completed

6. Children in college with variable rate student loans

Being in a financial bind certainly puts you at risk to lose equity in your home, and could put you in one of the worst loans: such as an Option ARM, Interest Only, 40-year mortgage or a home equity line of credit that will only increase your expenses further. Loan officers are trained to make money for their financial institutions and themselves. Therefore, you should be aware of the following sales scams:

1. An outright offer to refinance your mortgage into a 40-year loan package to lower your mortgage payment.

2. A hard push to get you to consolidate all of your debts including your car payments for a single low monthly payment.

3. You may have to accept a prepayment penalty to get the loan.

You should never accept any of these mortgage loan offers.

Follow these proven refinancing principles to mitigate your risks, and get the best loan:

1. Get the lowest interest rate possible that will lower your monthly payment, and add only five years to your loan. This means that the amount you added to your loan to refinance your mortgage will be paid off in five years.

2. **When you refinance your mortgage** you want to lower your monthly payment drastically from the amount you were paying. If your monthly reduction is only $50 after your loan calculation, that is not a meaningful reduction. A meaningful monthly payment reduction would be around $180 to $200.

3. **Depending on how many years you have left on your mortgage** you may want to refinance for 15 years as opposed to going back to 30 years. You would not get any benefit beyond the lower rate you receive. Always remember that decreasing you loan term is a good thing because time is against you.

4. **If you are underwater with credit card debt** and with interest payments as high as 28% or more, a single debt consolidation loan may be appropriate to get rid of this debt. However, you should make a commitment to yourself never to get into debt again.

5. **Be wary of reverse mortgages** Consult with a trusted real estate professional, financial advisor or estate planning attorney, who fully understands and can explain the risks and benefits of such a mortgage program.

Refinancing your home regularly is a bad practice. Every time you refinance your home you increase your mortgage debt and you certainly decrease your home equity. In addition, every time you refinance your home, depending on how many years you have paid the mortgage, you may start over with a 30-year mortgage loan or a 40-year loan. Aside from living in your home, you should always strive to accumulate some equity.

INVESTING

Please be aware of financial sales representatives who are trained to pry your savings away from you. These individuals will make impressive promises to you on how high your return will be if you invest a certain amount of money in their financial products. Be aware they never mention the risks associated with these products–one of which is losing most or all of your money. Please do not invest in any financial product that sounds too good to be true. Be vigilant and protect your finances from unscrupulous sales representatives.

The stock market is a dangerous investment vehicle. If you cannot afford to lose the money you are going to invest you should think long and hard before doing so. Bear in mind that you will never be able to beat the stock market and you should never try to do so. However, if you feel the urge to invest in stocks, you should seek out the services of a qualified broker and request that the broker purchases only inexpensive index funds or target date funds with very low expense ratio percentages. You should strive to pay as little in fees as possible.

If you are retired, be wary of the plethora of advertisements you receive from financial firms offering you a lunch or dinner to attend a seminar on various financial products that they will try to sell to you. You should attend these forums if you need information on financial products you would like to consider. However, you should not sign any forms. You should just listen to the information being presented, ask questions, get a business card and leave.

If you are working, you should strive to take advantage of the tax benefits offered for 401(k) and IRA accounts. If you can, you should maximize your saving for these accounts as much as possible. Remember when you retire you will be in a lower tax bracket. If you want additional tax savings, you should invest in a Roth 401(k) or a Roth IRA.

40

CHAPTER 7

ESTATE PLANNING STRATEGIES

The strategies presented here for estate planning is to educate families and individuals on the actions they will have to take to complete the planning process, and be ready for life changing events. *These are very complicated actions, and should be done only with the help of an experienced estate planning attorney.* The estate planning actions are enumerated as follows:

1. **Create a Health Care Power of Attorney:** things happen in life when you least expect them to occur that may leave you unable to make vital life decisions for yourself. Do not allow these decisions to be made by someone you do not know. Therefore, you need to set up a health care power of attorney that gives an individual you have selected and designated to make medical decisions that you would have made on your behalf. This is a very personal decision, and should be made with certainty that the individual you choose would be committed and willing to follow your requests without finding the decision

making process too onerous. Once you have made a selection let the person know that decisions may have to be made for home health care, nursing home care, organ donation, how you want to be treated if you cannot communicate, do you want to have any restrictions or wishes such as receiving CPR and being placed on a ventilator. Indicate if you want to receive traditional or alternative forms of medical treatment and use of technology. *To complete the power of attorney designation, obtain a power of attorney form from your state's website and follow the instructions. If you do not complete your health care power of attorney form, your designation could be invalid.*

2. **Create a Living Will:** the health care power of attorney gives families or designee the power to authorize medical decisions on your behalf. The living will works in conjunction with the power of attorney to create advanced medical directives. This allows your family or agent to follow your wishes to the letter. *Follow these strategies for your living will:*

   • *Select someone you have confidence in* and trust to make decisions about your care if you are unable to do so.

   • *Have a frank conversation with your designee* about the type of medical treatments you prefer.

   • *Make certain that the person you choose* will be able to carry out your wishes despite the emotional and psychological toll that will be evident.

Once all forms have been witnessed and notarized, provide copies to your health care professionals, the person you designated to make decisions and close family members.

3. Power of Attorney: A power of attorney is a document that gives a person the authority to carry out on your behalf your financial and business affairs (known as your Attorney-in-Fact). This person will have the authority to make binding legal and financial decisions on your behalf. Your selection should be someone who is honest and financially secure. However, keep in mind that even honest people have financial problems and can easily be tempted when money is involved. Be careful when assigning power of attorney to relatives or friends who are unreliable. Remember, the power of attorney document becomes invalid upon your death. Therefore, you should be vigilant and ensure that you will have specific instructions on how your estate should be divided or administered. Your **43** Attorney-in-Fact will have the following responsibilities:

- *Pay every day expenses*
- *File and pay taxes*
- *Invest your retirement funds*
- *Hire attorney to represent you in court*
- *Sell your property, such as a car and home*
- *Sign contract or legal documents*

4. Executing Your Power of Attorney

There are two types of power of attorney

- *Durable Power of Attorney:* This document is effective immediately and remains in effect even if you become incapacitated due to a serious medical condition.

- *A Springing Power of Attorney:* A Springing Power of Attorney 'springs' to life upon your incapacitation. Your agent may have to prove that you are incapacitated, which may cause delay and interfere with the management of your affairs.

REVIEW YOUR ASSETS

Review your assets to make certain you have incorporated all the changes that have taken place in your investment or retirement accounts as you calculate your net worth. You will need this information when you create your will.

REVIEW BENEFICIARIES

Now is the time to write a will to take control of your life. If you fail to have a will, the state in which you reside will take control and determine how your assets will be distributed and who will raise your children. *Remember to update your beneficiaries before you make a will, because beneficiaries' designations or legatees will override a will.* Review your 401(k) account, insurance policies and retirement accounts and make changes to beneficiaries if necessary.

44

Making a will allows you to designate a person *(executor)* to handle your estate when you die. The will directs how your property will be managed and distributed. The will allows you to name a guardian for minor children and dependents. *Note: should you die without a will it is called intestacy. Your estate will be administered by state laws on descent and distribution.* When you die without a will it takes longer to adjudicate your affairs, so make certain you have a will. Remember for a will to be valid it must be signed in front of two witnesses. The witnesses should not be one of your beneficiaries; this could make the will invalid.

The executor of your will should be a person you trust; please select with care. If your affairs are complicated, you should name an attorney or a professional to administer your estate. Make certain that you state specifically that your executor has power to pay your bills. In addition, specify how your assets should be distributed among your loved ones to prevent squabbles over your estate. Spouses should not have joint wills. It is better to deal with ex-spouses and children in your own will.

We all live very busy lives dealing with daily challenges. Providing for our families needs, working one or two jobs to increase our income, educating our children, providing health care and housing for our family and taking care of a family member who is in poor health fill our lives. Performing all of these tasks can be very stressful. Many of us forget to take the necessary actions needed to deal with life changing events. *I strongly urge everyone reading this book to get these documents completed for their own benefit and the benefit of their families.*

CONCLUSION

Do not allow yourself to become a victim of the daily barrage of advertisements soliciting you to spend money. This book provides you with the basic principles and a road map to become financially secure. However, I could not finish writing this book without telling a personal story. My good friends John and Mary, both medical doctors and a married couple, are two beautiful individuals who have achieved social and financial success in their lives. Due to extravagant spending they found themselves in severe financial difficulties. The level of debt accumulated indicates a lack of financial discipline, and further illustrates that extravagant spending affects many of us regardless of the level of education or social and economic status. Remember when you accumulate debt you have to pay it off. You lose time trying to improve your financial position. When it comes to saving money, time is your enemy; once you lose time you never get it back. The essential principles enumerated in this book are the building blocks for achieving financial empowerment, economic growth and economic stability in the lives of families and individuals.

My hope is that if you have struggled with financial challenges, you will find this book an invaluable resource and begin the journey of working towards fulfilling your dream of achieving permanent wealth and prosperity.

APPENDIX A

SAMPLE PROMISSORY NOTE

46

PROMISSORY NOTE

$_____(AMOUNT) _____(DATE)

FOR VALUE RECEIVED, the undersigned, (the "Maker"), hereby promises to pay to the order of_____ (LENDER NAME) ("Payee"), the principal sum of $ _____ pursuant to the terms and conditions set forth herein.

PAYMENT OF PRINCIPAL. The principal amount of this Promissory Note (the "Note") and any accrued but unpaid interest shall be due and payable in _____ (NUMBER OF PAYMENTS) (CIRCLE ONE: equal monthly installments / equal quarterly installments / payments as described below) beginning _____ (DATE OF FIRST PAYMENT). All payments under this Note shall be applied first to accrued but unpaid interest, and next to outstanding principal. If not sooner paid, the entire remaining indebtedness (including accrued interest) shall be due and payable on _____ (DATE OF FINAL PAYMENT).

INTEREST. This Note shall bear interest, compounded annually, at _____ (ANNUAL INTEREST RATE) percent.

PREPAYMENT. The Maker shall have the right at any time and from time to time to prepay this Note in whole or in part without premium or penalty.

REMEDIES. No delay or omission on part of the holder of this Note in exercising any right hereunder shall operate as a waiver of any such right or of any other right of such holder, nor shall any delay, omission or waiver on any one occasion be deemed a bar to or waiver of the same or any other right on any future occasion. The rights and remedies of the Payee shall be cumulative and may be pursued singly, successively, or together, in the sole discretion of the Payee.

EVENTS OF ACCELERATION. The occurrence of any of the following shall constitute an "Event of Acceleration" by Maker under this Note: (a) Maker's failure to pay any part of the principal or interest as and when due under this Note; or (b) Maker's becoming insolvent or not paying its debts as they become due.

ACCELERATION. Upon the occurrence of an Event of Acceleration under this Note, and in addition to any other rights and remedies that Payee may have, Payee shall have the right, at its sole and exclusive option, to declare this Note immediately due and payable.

SUBORDINATION. The Maker's obligations under this Promissory Note are subordinated to all indebtedness, if any, of Maker, to any unrelated third party lender to the extent such indebtedness is outstanding on the date of this Note and such subordination is required under the loan documents providing for such indebtedness.

WAIVERS BY MAKER. All parties to this Note including Maker and any sureties, endorsers, and guarantors hereby waive protest, presentment, notice of dishonor, and notice of acceleration of maturity and agree to continue to remain bound for the payment of principal, interest and all other sums due under this Note notwithstanding any change or changes by way of release, surrender, exchange, modification or substitution of any security for this Note or by way of any extension or extensions of time for the payment of principal and interest; and all such parties waive all and every kind of notice of such change or changes and agree that the same may be made without notice or consent of any of them.

EXPENSES. In the event any payment under this Note is not paid when due, the Maker agrees to pay, in addition to the principal and interest hereunder, reasonable attorneys' fees not exceeding a sum equal to 15% of the then outstanding balance owing on the Note, plus all other reasonable expenses incurred by Payee in exercising any of its rights and remedies upon default.

GOVERNING LAW. This Note shall be governed by, and construed in accordance with, the laws of the State of _____ (STATE NAME).

48

SUCCESSORS. All of the foregoing is the promise of Maker and shall bind Maker and Maker's successors, heirs and assigns; provided, however, that Maker may not assign any of its rights or delegate any of its obligations hereunder without the prior written consent of the holder of this Note.

IN WITNESS WHEREOF, Maker has executed this Promissory Note as of the day and year first above written.

Maker:_____
(BORROWER SIGNATURE)

_____
(BORROWER NAME)

INDEX

50

51

54